Copyright © 2018 by Larry Zielke
Story Editor R. Fernandez
All Rights Reserved
Art by Herald Entertainment, Inc.
Printed in China
First Printing: June 2018
ISBN: 978-1-947774-75-9

THE ZooMaster
from MARS

Written by Larry Zielke

Zoo-Master came from planet Mars
And brought his zoo in little jars.
Each creature different, none quite the same;
Some were wild, but most were tame.

Like a talking book, the Silly-sage
Each day of his life grows another page.
One thousand eyes has the Tattle-tate;
Each eye pops out to investigate.

There's the Snip-ett, the Snup-ett,
The Snazz and the Snee,
The Cringe and the Crup-ett,
The Dazz and the Dee.

But the strangest of all you can't help but view,
'Cause it makes itself look just like me or you,
Is the one that we stared at— the See-Me-Elf.
When I looked at him, all I saw was myself!

He spoke our language, he learned it when
He was just a wee elf of nine or ten.
From books and papers, videos and tapes
Astronauts had left in outer space.

"You are so handsome," the elf said with a grin.
I didn't know if he meant me or him.
So I said with a smile, "You are too!"
"Well, of course," he replied. "I look just like you!"

His cheerfulness made him an instant star
Making each of us happy to be who we are.

He said, "Look in the mirror and you will see
That just being yourself is the best thing to be!"

"Just don't be like the Kopy-err, whose goal is to be,
Him, her, they, or you—anyone but me!
You can't be someone else, so it really is best
To work on becoming your most You-I-Est!"

Something to Talk About

- What do you like about this story and why?

- What do you think See-Me-Elf was trying to teach the children in the story?

- What do you think it means to 'be true to yourself'?

- Who is your favorite zoo creature in the story? On a separate sheet, draw your favorite zoo creature.

Copyright © 2018 by By Larry Zielke
Story Editor R. Fernandez
All Rights Reserved
Art by Herald Entertainment, Inc.
Printed in China
First Printing: June 2018
ISBN: 978-1-947774-75-9

Make-believe stories are a fun way to entertain children while teaching them to make right choices in real life situations.

"The ZooMaster from Mars"
▼
Helps children be content with who they are, and not to compare themselves negatively with others

"Don't Ever Park Your Camel on a Busy, Crowded Street"
▼
Teaches children to respect others, even those they may not know.

For more information please visit:
www.LZBooks.com